Build Your Colonial Dollhouse

Plan Book: 9 Room Colonial Doll House

By Dollhouse Devotions

All rights reserved.

No part of this publication may be reproduced in any form or by any means, including scanning, photocopying, or otherwise without prior written permission of the copyright holder.

Disclaimer and Terms of Use: The Author and Publisher has strived to be as accurate and complete as possible in the creation of this book, notwithstanding the fact that he does not warrant or represent at any time that the contents within are accurate due to the rapidly changing nature of the Internet. While all attempts have been made to verify information provided in this publication, the Author and Publisher assumes no responsibility for errors, omissions, or contrary interpretation of the subject matter herein.

As with any craft book, care needs to be taken when working with anything sharp, chemical based or anything else craft related. The Author and Publisher are not responsible for any injury relating to the use of craft supplies.

You are given a non-transferable, "personal use" license to this product. You cannot distribute it or share it with other individuals.

Also, there are no resale rights or private label rights granted when purchasing this document. In other words, it's for your own personal use only.

The original illustrations and plans for this book came from the book 'The Boy Craftsman'. Additional illustrations and updated instructions have been provided by Dollhouse Devotions.

Build Your Own Colonial Dollhouse

Plan Book: 9 Room Colonial Doll House

By Dollhouse Devotions

Table of Contents

Introduction 7
General Instructions 10

    Patterns 10
    Foam Core 11
    Wood 11
    Nails 12
    Illustration Board 13
    Turnings 14
    Trim 16

Colonial House 17

    Important Info: 18
    First Floor 21
    First Floor Partitions 23
    Stairs 25
    Railings 32
    Outer Walls 34
    Second Floor 36
    Third-Floor 40
    The House Ends 43
    Roof 44
    Windows 50
    Front Steps 54

Finishing Touches 59

    Floors 59
    Wall Pictures 61
    Brick 62
    Shingles 63
    Stained Glass 64
    Wallpaper 64

Introduction

From simple one-room cottages, to log cabins, to Colleen Moore's Fairy Tale Castle, there's just something about a dollhouse that appeals to the child in us all.

In days gone by, the dollhouse was a true work of art, something you would be proud to display to friends and family. They were the realms of adults, not children.

These days, there are more 'kit' houses available than ever before. However, the modern miniaturist isn't looking for a kit house. The dollhouse collector and artist wants something more challenging, more inspirational.

They want something more like the dollhouses of days gone by. They want a dollhouse that's a work of art.

This book series will introduce you to some of the most popular and the most unusual dollhouses of days gone by.

These books have been specially designed to look like a plan book from yesteryear. From their creamy papers to their charming hand drawn illustrations, to their faux woven cover, everything is designed to give you an experience like few other books can.

Important info will be at the beginning of each project. It will give you a list of materials, the difficulty level, the size of the house according to the measurements and how easy it can be replicated in foam core.

At the end of each book there are some easy decorating ideas such as hardwood floors and carpets and shingles.

Every lover of dollhouses wants a dollhouse as beautiful and unique as the treasures it contains and this book will provide hours of fun as you create the perfect dollhouse for all your treasures.

****

As a crafter and dollhouse lover myself, I know what a hassle it is to try to copy patterns out of books.

That's why I've included a link that enables you to download all the patterns in this book in reduced size PDF form.

You can use your computer or copier to adjust them to whatever size you need.

Simply scan the QR code below or go to this website to get your PDF patterns:

http://www.thisofferisgreat.com/dhcolonial

General Instructions

Patterns

This book contains patterns and illustrations for all the dollhouses.

The patterns in this series come in a variety sizes. While many are for 1:12 houses, others are not.

Fortunately, you can actually make these houses any size you want by making minor adjustments and enlarging the pattern to the size you need.

While measurements don't need to be quite as exact as the ones given here, precise measurements do give a wonderful 'starting point' for your ultimate creation.

Foam Core

Though traditional dollhouses are made of wood, I have always preferred foam core due to its ease of use. The instructions for each house are for wood. However, they can also be made out of foam core with relative ease. For each house, I mention the level of difficulty involved with following the instructions to turn it into a foam core house rather than a wooden one.

Wood

It all starts with the wood. What kind of wood you choose is ultimately decided by what kind of dollhouse you want. A dollhouse that will be completely covered in wallpaper and brick can use very rough wood, such as plywood. However, a dollhouse that's going to be finely finished and painted should use a wood of higher quality.

The highest quality wood for dollhouses is basswood. Even though it's among the most expensive, the finished result is truly an heirloom quality house.

If price is a concern, you can choose less-expensive wood, like pine. Pine can still give you a finely finished heirloom quality dollhouse for a fraction of the cost of basswood. Additionally, being a soft wood, it's still very easy to work with.

The most important thing to remember when working with pine or other woods is to make sure it's free from knots and other out of scale defects that could ruin the overall look of your perfect house.

Nails

Because this is not a real house, we can use smaller nails that leave easy to fill holes.

While screws will give you the sturdiest house, finishing nails will give you an overall smooth appearance and can be punched in with an awl.

Once punched in, finishing nails are easily covered up with a little bit of wood putty, sandpaper and paint.

Illustration Board

Illustration board is available at many fine art stores and is wonderful for a variety of purposes. Illustration board is actually a type of compressed cardboard. It is sturdy and easy to cut with a craft knife.

Illustration board is easy to curve around things. To curve illustration board, use a craft knife to lightly score the illustration board as shown by the dotted lines below.

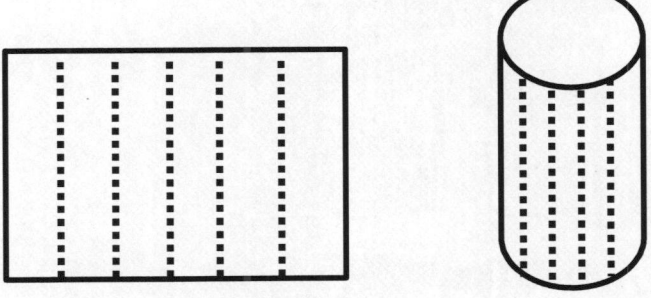

Once you've scored the illustration board, curve the illustration board away from the lines instead of toward.

This method can be used for creating columns, arches, tubes and bowed windows.

Cardstock can then be wrapped around the piece and finished as desired.

Turnings

Throughout this book, you'll notice references to 'turnings'. Turnings are fancy, 3 dimensional, freestanding, carved woodwork.

Example of turnings

Turnings can be used in a variety of places in your dollhouse, including:

- Stair railings
- Poster Beds
- Architectural columns
- Furniture legs
- More…

In this book, we use them primarily for creating railings for stairs.

Real wood turnings can be bought relatively cheaply at just about any dollhouse supply store or catalogue.

You can find a section of online resources in the back of the books where you can buy turnings.

However, for the truly creative, you can use beads to simulate wood turnings.

These beads can be either wood or plastic. Carved beads, such as ethnic beads make a particularly good looking carved 'turning'.

Simply stack beads on top of each other until you get the size and shape that you want. Glue them in place. Then paint the beads to resemble wood.

Just like with wood turnings, these bead 'turnings' can give you a wonderful effect and can be used for furniture feet, elaborate carvings, columns and posters on a four poster

Turning made from beads

bed.

Trim

Trim can go either on the inside or outside of the dollhouse. It can be the molding next to the floorboards, the ceiling or the outside of the house.

It can also go around the windows, doors and porches.

Though you can buy regular wood trim from your favorite dollhouse retailer, there are other ways to simulate trim.

Heavily textured lace or embossed papers work well as trim. In addition, lace has the added benefit of being able to bend around curves and corners without needing to be mitered.

Deeply Etched Lace

Heavily textured lace, like the lace in the picture, works best for this.

Colonial House

A COLONIAL DOLLHOUSE

Important Info:

Size of house:

- 30" L X 20" D X 3' H.

Level of difficulty:

- Easy to intermediate

Can be reproduced in foam core:

- Easily

Materials:

- Sheets of wood (and tools for wood)
- Glue
- Strip wood
- Plastic sheet glass
- Toothpicks/dowels
- Illustration board (board)
- Cardstock (Card)
- T-square (or carpenters ruler)
- Pencil

The colonial house is one of the easiest homes to make. Colonial homes were largely symmetrical. They were also boxy with few adornments or architectural features.

This house will be a rather large dollhouse. It has three floors, nine rooms and sides that fold out for easy access.

Once you master building this house, you'll be ready for the more challenging houses in this series.

This house starts with the false basement. This basement also creates the base.

To make it look like a real basement, we will be adding small faux windows with grating over them.

The base is actually not sitting on a board. Instead, it's raised up off the ground by building a framework of strips of wood as shown in the illustration.

Cut wood strips from your large sheet of wood, strips about 4" high. The ones on the long side should be 30" while the ones on the short side should be 20".

There is no need to miter the edges as the basement will be completely covered by brick work.

Simply glue or nail the 4 strips together as you would a box.

First Floor

Cut out a piece of wood the size and shape needed for the first floor. It's better for the floor to overlap slightly then to be cut too short.

Using figure 65 as a guide, mark off where the partitions and stairs go.

A T-square or some other type of carpenter's ruler will give you the straightest partition marks.

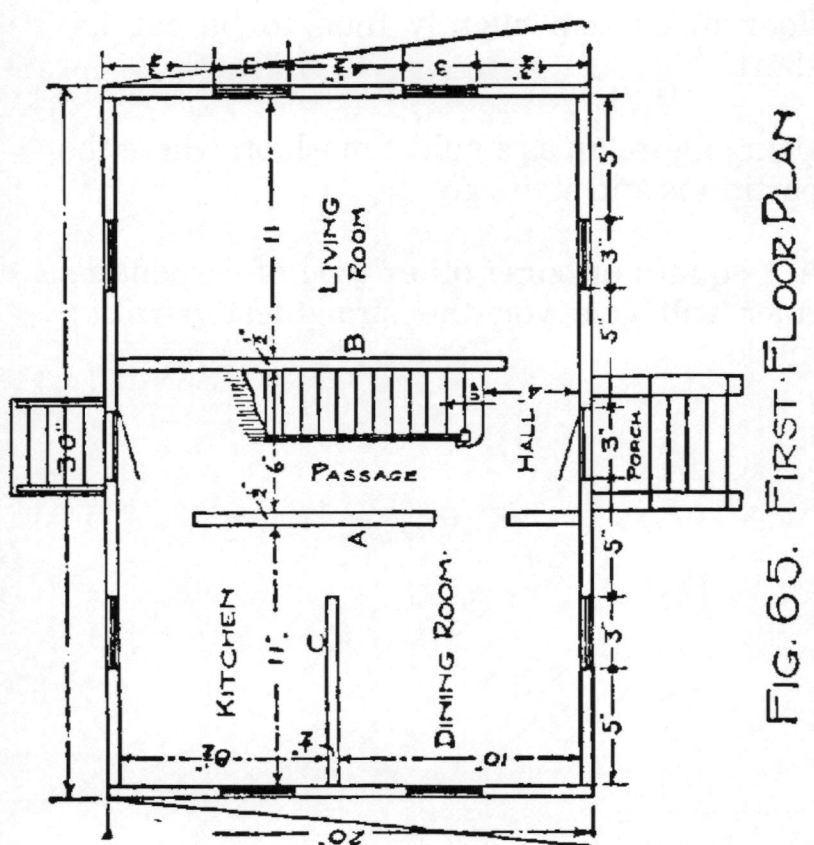

Fig. 65. First Floor Plan

First Floor Partitions

Partitions in this house are easier to set up floor by floor before the outside walls go up.

There are three partitions for the first floor; A, B and C. Use the patterns to cut them the same size and shape as shown in figure 68.

Once you have these partitions cut, attach them to the floor using screws, nails or glue. A carpenter's square will help ensure that your partition walls stay straight.

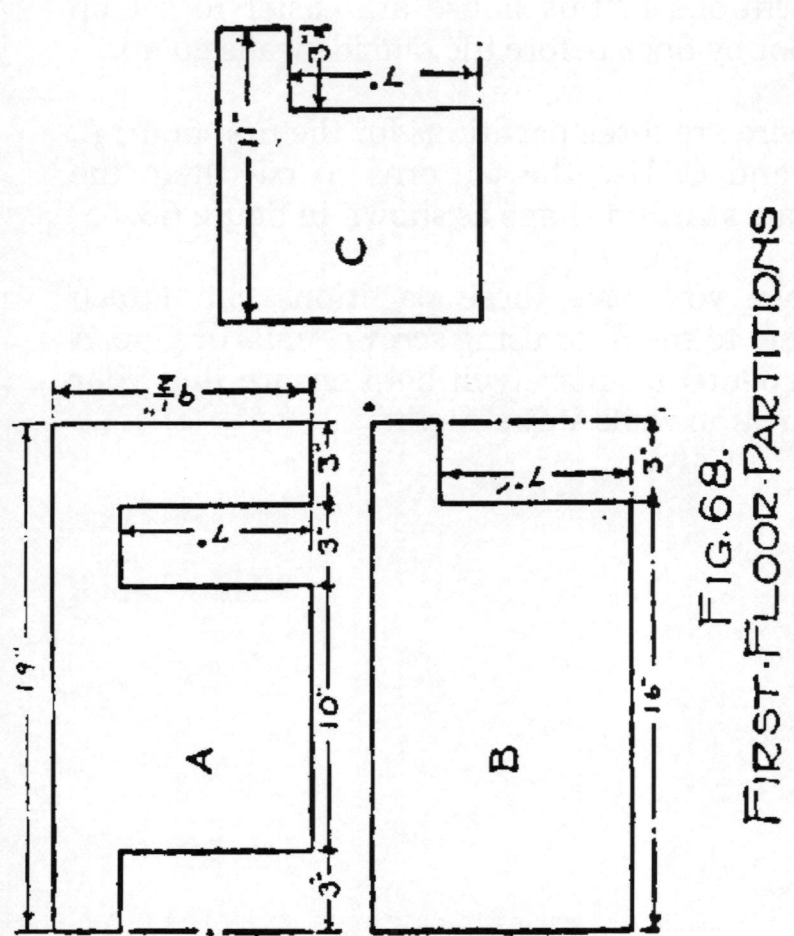

Fig. 68.
First·Floor·Partitions

24

Stairs

Working on the stairs before the outer walls and other floors go up is easier than trying to fit them in place later.

The stairs will be laid as we lay the floors. However, these instructions are for all the stairs in the house.

Making all the stairs now will enable you to have them available when you are ready for them.

When it comes to stairs, some technical terminology is needed. These are the words that will be used often throughout the rest of this book.

Stairs have three main parts: stringers risers and treads.
'Treads' are the top part of the stairs or where the foot goes.

'Risers' are the parts of the stairs that lift the treads up from the step below it.

'Stringers' are the sides of the stairs.

They support both the treads and risers. Together, these pieces make up the steps.

Trace the pattern of figure 73 onto a piece of illustration board. This is known as the 'pitch board'. Pitch boards help create the pattern for ensuring the stairs are even and perfect.

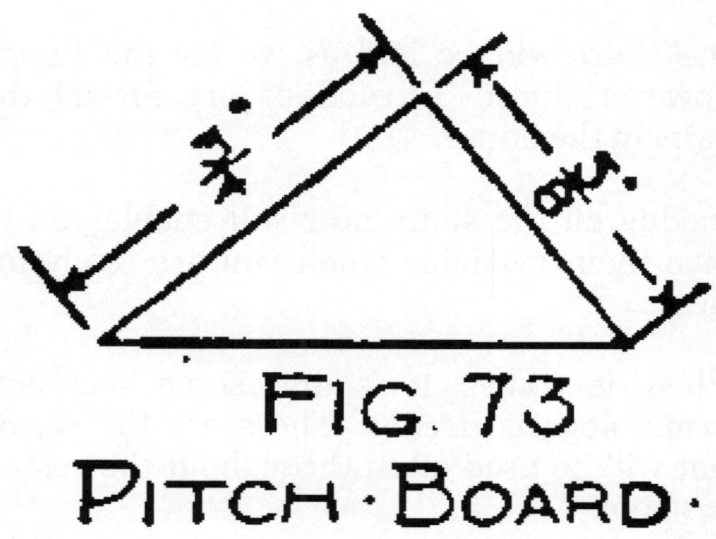

FIG. 73
PITCH·BOARD·

Prepare two stringers for each flight of stairs.

Both stories have 16 stairs.

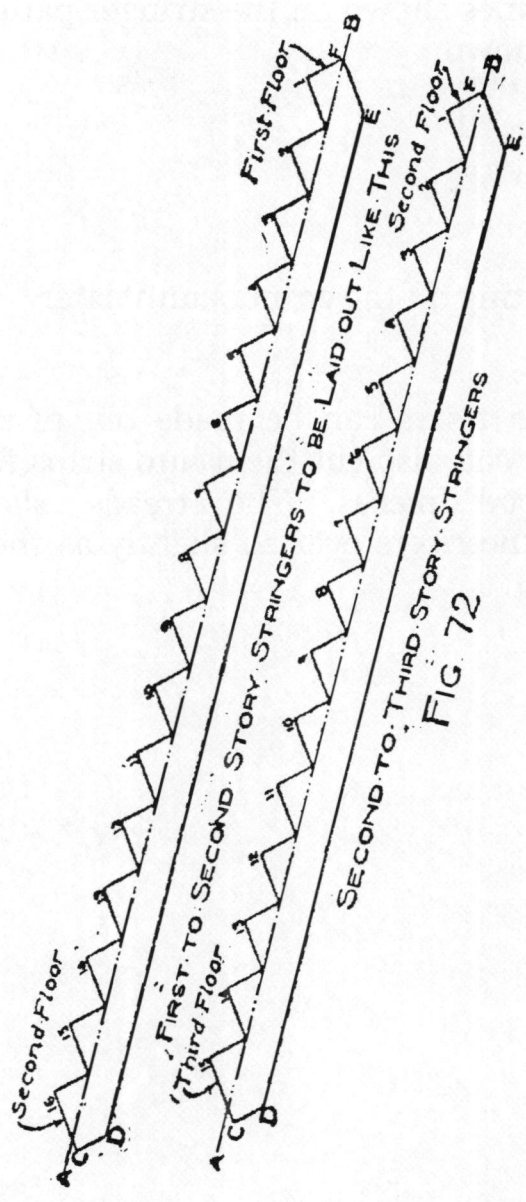

Fig. 72

Draw the lines shown on the stringer patterns above as shown:

- DE to AB
- CD to EF

Leave splitting off the corners until later.

Treads and risers can be made out of strip wood. You can also cut them into strips from larger wood pieces. The treads should overhang the risers ever so slightly as shown in figure 74.

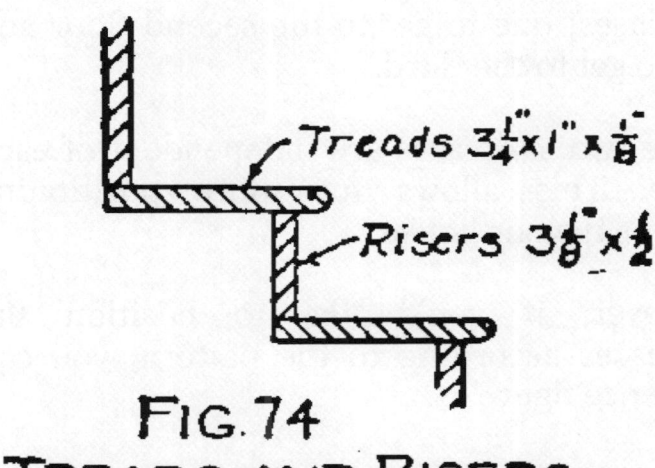

FIG. 74
TREADS AND RISERS.

Since stairs are too delicate for nails, the treads and risers are attached to the stringers using glue.

Use the pitch board to ensure that all the stairs are the same size and elevation. If one stair must be of slightly higher or lower elevation, the bottom stair can be used for this purpose.

Upon finishing, you should have two staircases; one to get to the second floor and one to get to the third.

These two staircases are independent of each other. This allows for more positioning options in your house.

However, if you'd like to position the staircases according to the pattern, you can reference figure 71.

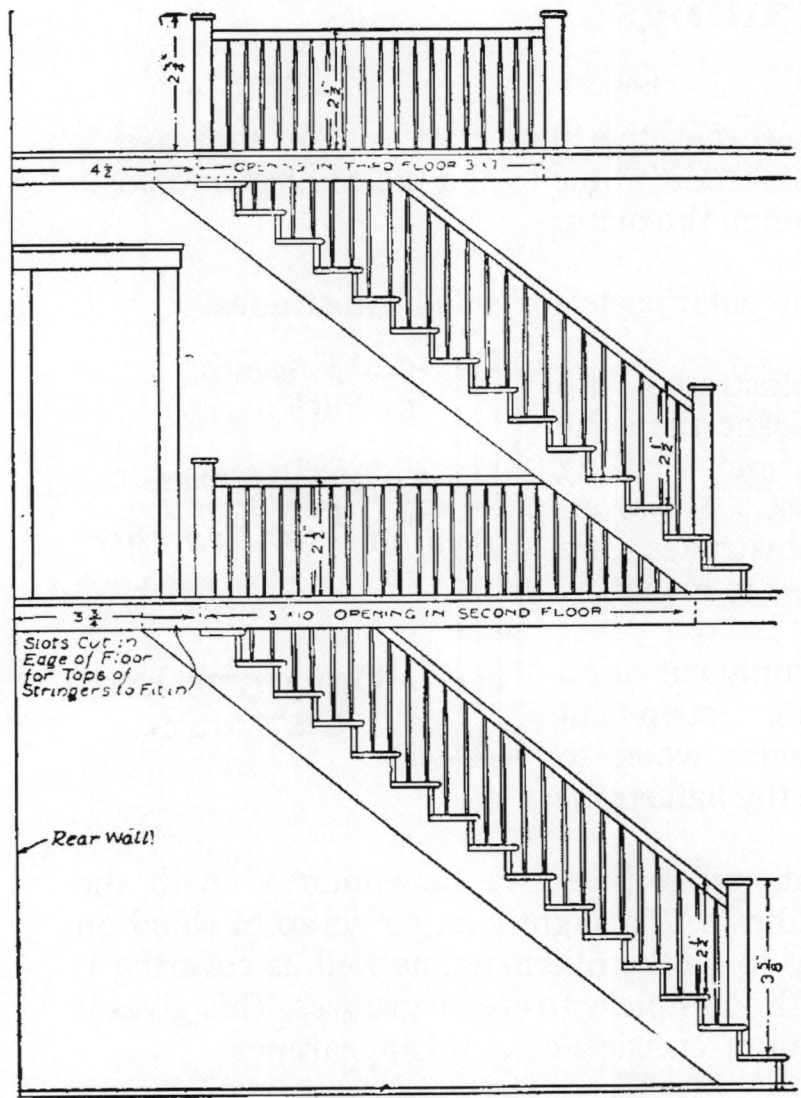

FIG. 71. — Details of Inside Stairs.

Railings

Now that the stair part of the staircase is finished, it's time to add the railings and posts seen in the picture.

The pillar posts are called balustrades.

Balustrades are thicker than the normal railing post. However, balustrades are easy to make.

Simply cut out a long strip of square wood to be the balustrade.

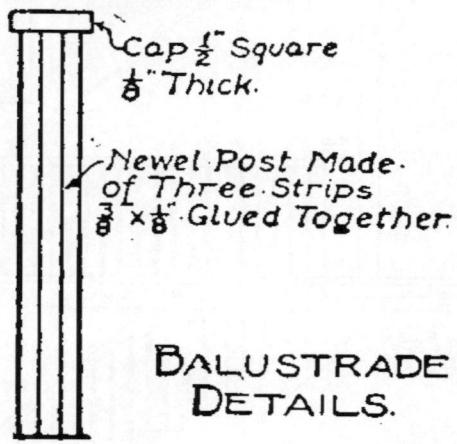

This pillar post can be enhanced with the addition of a slightly larger scrap of wood on top to be the overhang, as well as covering it with toothpicks to create grooves. This gives it a more 'classical column' appearance.

Additionally, you can also use pieces of strip wood or bead 'turnings' to create balustrades.

Because of the delicacy, the turnings that make up the posts between the balustrades are nothing more than simple toothpicks.

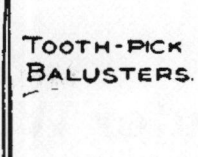

You can use round toothpicks, square craft sticks or even carved toothpicks to get the effect you want.

Simply cut them to size and glue them to the stairs.

The railing is made out of a piece of strip wood or skewer.

If possible, you can cut a groove into the top of the railing to keep the toothpicks in line and hide flaws in the height.

If that is not possible, a very thin piece of stripwood or lace trim could work here.

Outer Walls

Once the stairs are completed, you can start on the rest of the house.

The outer walls, the front and rear, go up next. The included pattern can be used for both the front and the rear.

Colonial homes were very symmetrical.

The outer walls should be 29"wide and 20" high.

The window openings should also be cut at this time.

Regular house windows are 3" x 5" and start 2" above the floor.

The basement windows will be 2" x 3".

The doorways, both front and back, measure 3" x 7."

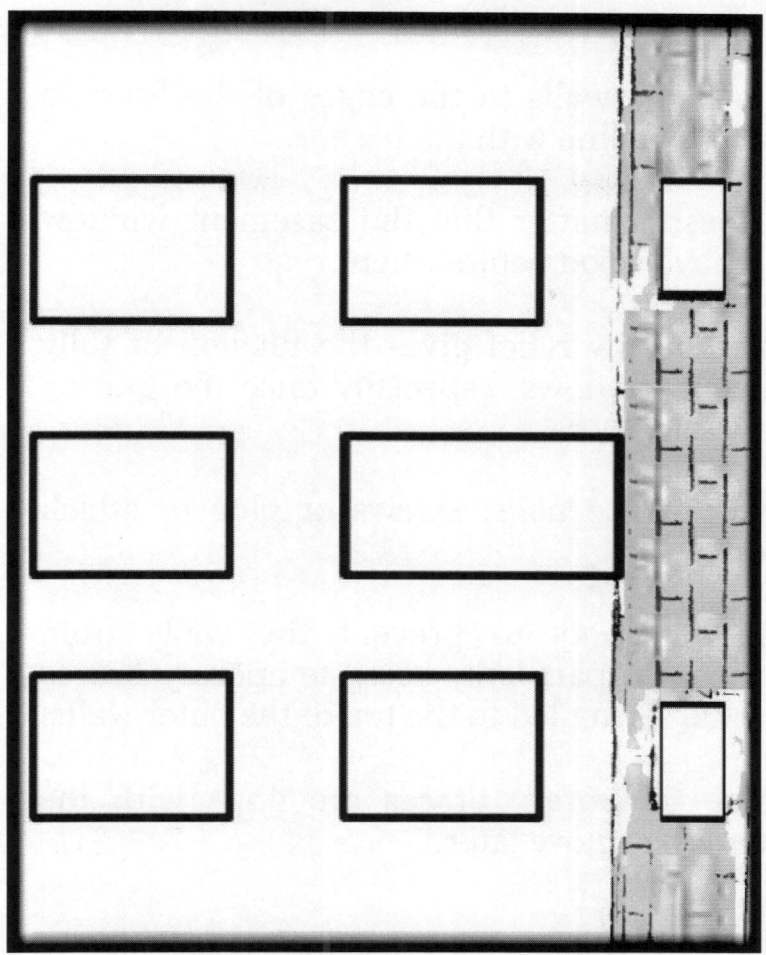

35

Attach the walls to the edges of the floor so they are in line with the base.

It doesn't matter that the basement window will have wood behind them.

This shallow relief gives the illusion of fully formed windows, especially once the grating is in place.

You can use nails, screws or glue to attach these walls.

The best way to prevent the walls from spreading apart is by using temporary braces that can be nailed to the top of the outer walls.

These temporary braces are done with the intent to remove later.

Second Floor

Unlike the first floor, this floor starts by cutting the opening for the stairs.

This opening will be 3" x 10". It will be positioned on the spot indicated in figure 66.

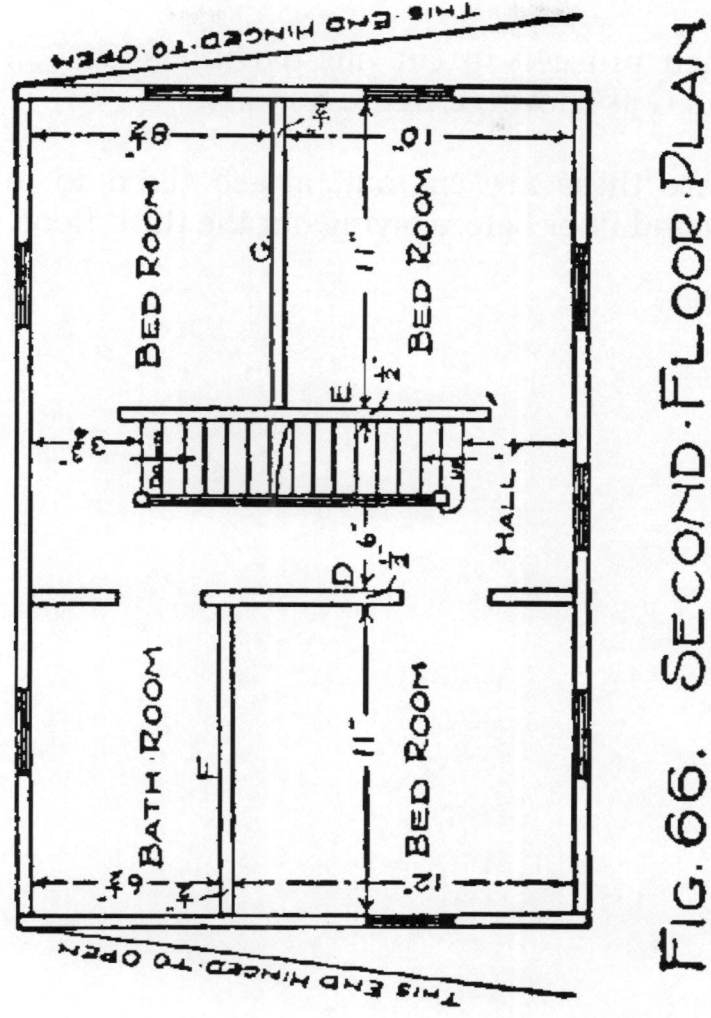

Mark the location of the partitions using figure 66.

Then proceed to cut out partitions D, E, F, and G as shown in figure 69.

Once these are cut out, attach them to the second floor before laying out the third floor.

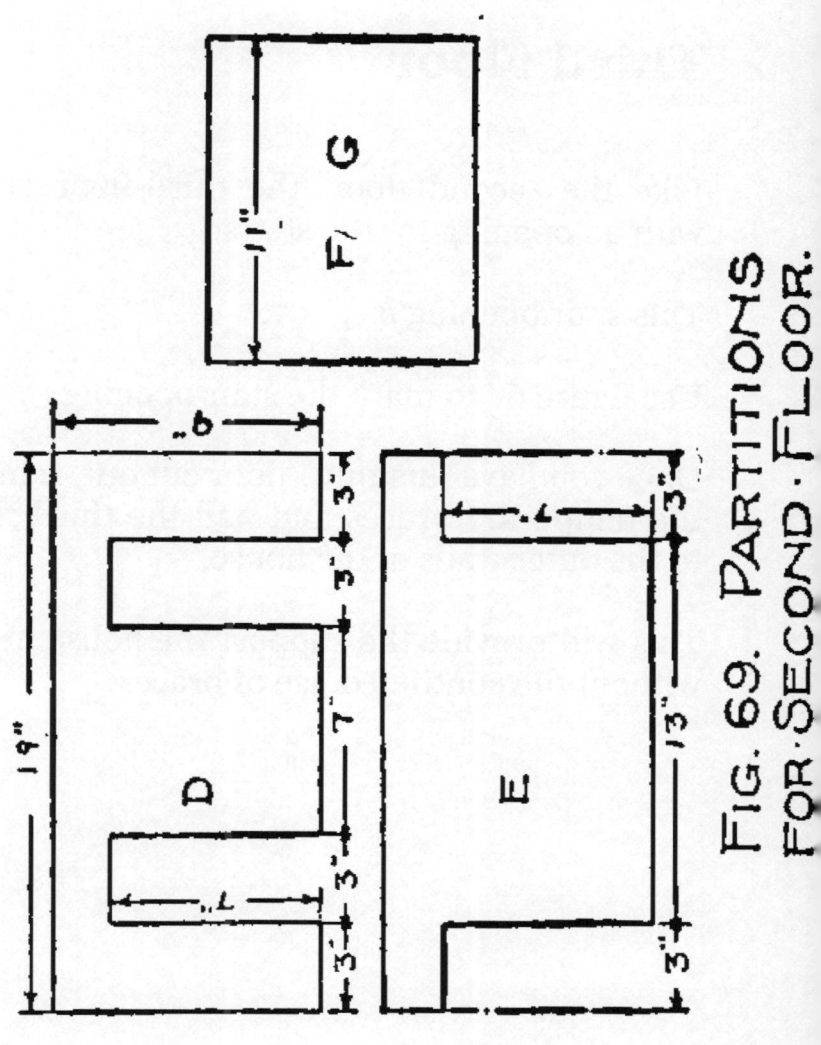

FIG. 69. PARTITIONS FOR SECOND FLOOR.

Third Floor

Like the second floor, the third-floor starts with an opening for the stairs.

This stair opening is 3" x 7."

Use figure 67 to mark the stair opening.

Once you have this third floor cut out, remove the temporary braces and nail the third floor to the outer walls of the house.

This will provide the support the house needs without the continued use of braces.

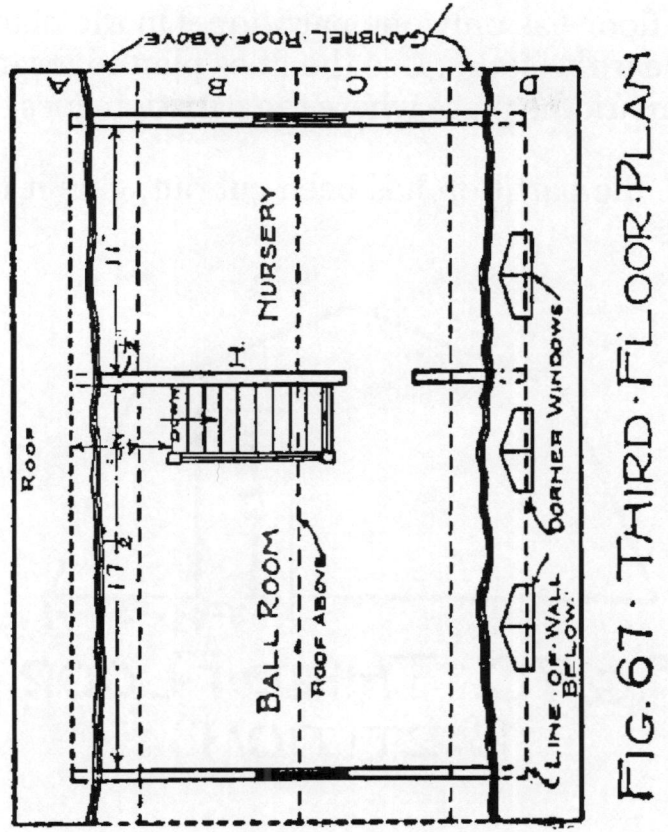

This floor has only one partition. On the plan, it's near the stairs. Use the floor plan to locate and mark the place where the partition goes.

Once the partition has been cut out, glue it in place.

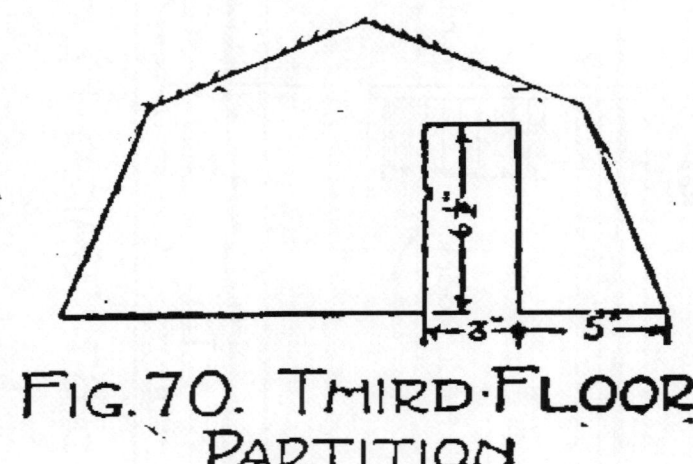

Fig. 70. Third Floor Partition

The House Ends

The ends of the house are easy to make.

They are simply two pieces of wood, 20" square.

A cabinet hinge placed at the top and bottom of will enable the sides to open.

A cabinet hook-and-eye latch will enable you to close the dollhouse when not in use.

Roof

This roof is slightly more challenging than normal roofs. That's because it is not made up of two square pieces; it's made up of four.
Many colonial houses were done in this style of roof. It was known as a Gambrel Roof.

The roof itself is not difficult. It is made up of four pieces of wood. The first piece is 8"h x 34"l. The second piece is 9"h x 34"l.

The gable ends are the ends of the house that attach to the roof.

The easiest and most precise way to make the gables is to reference figure 77 and use a compass to create a circle 20" in diameter.

Next, mark out the octagon shape as shown in figure 77.

Remove all the curved edges using the straight lines you made. the octagon shapes is shown in figure 77 until you have an octagon.

Then, cut the octagon into two halves.

These will be your gable ends.

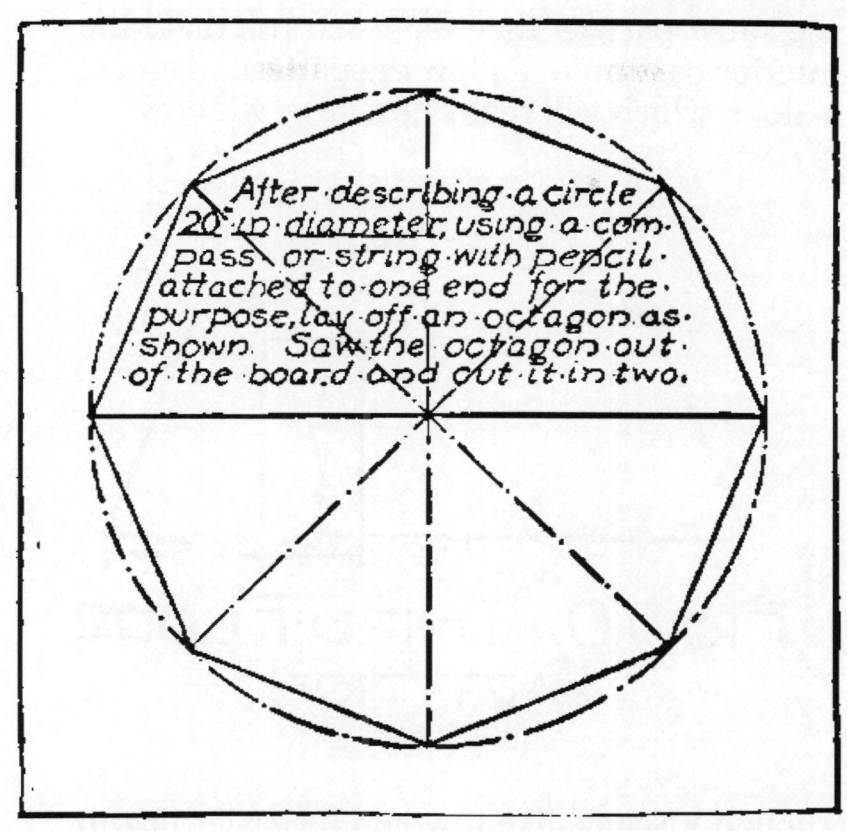

FIG. 77. — Make Gable-ends like This.

Windows for the gable ends are created using the same pattern that was used to create the interior partition. Follow the pattern to create a 'door' which will really be a large window.

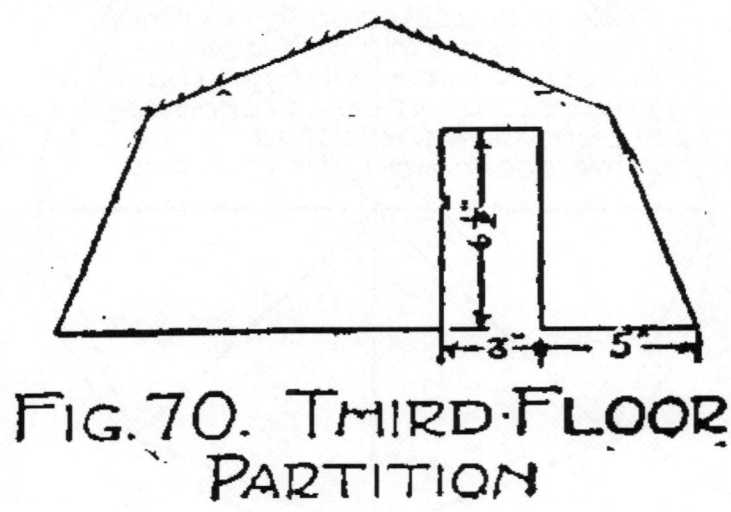

FIG. 70. THIRD·FLOOR PARTITION

Though it seems like it would be easier just to use the pattern for the interior partition as the gable ends, using the octagon method gives a more precise fit.

Upper roof parts, B and C, should overlap slightly over each gable.

Hinges to the upper parts of the roof, A and D, attach to the lower roof parts of B and C.

The addition of these hinges allows you access to the third-floor.

If working with wood, you might have to bevel the edges and do a little bit of sanding and fitting in order to make the hinged roof work and fit as it should. This can take a little bit of time, but is very important.

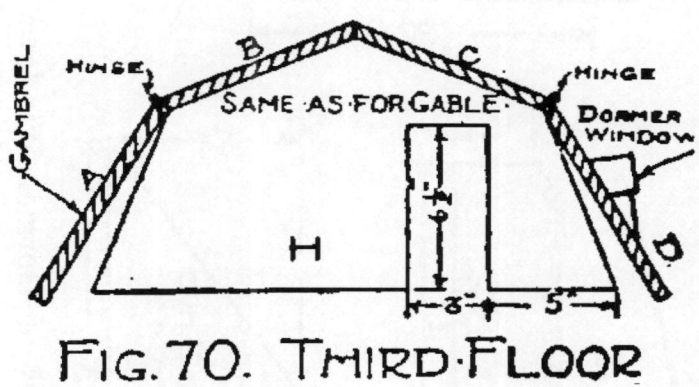

FIG. 70. THIRD·FLOOR

Dormer Windows

Dormer windows are designed to fit over the hinged part of the roof. They go directly over the middle of the regular windows.

To create dormer windows, use the patterns given in figures 80, 81 and 82. Cut out the following pieces:

- Shape A: 6 Pieces
- Shape B: 3 Pieces
- Shape C: 6 Pieces

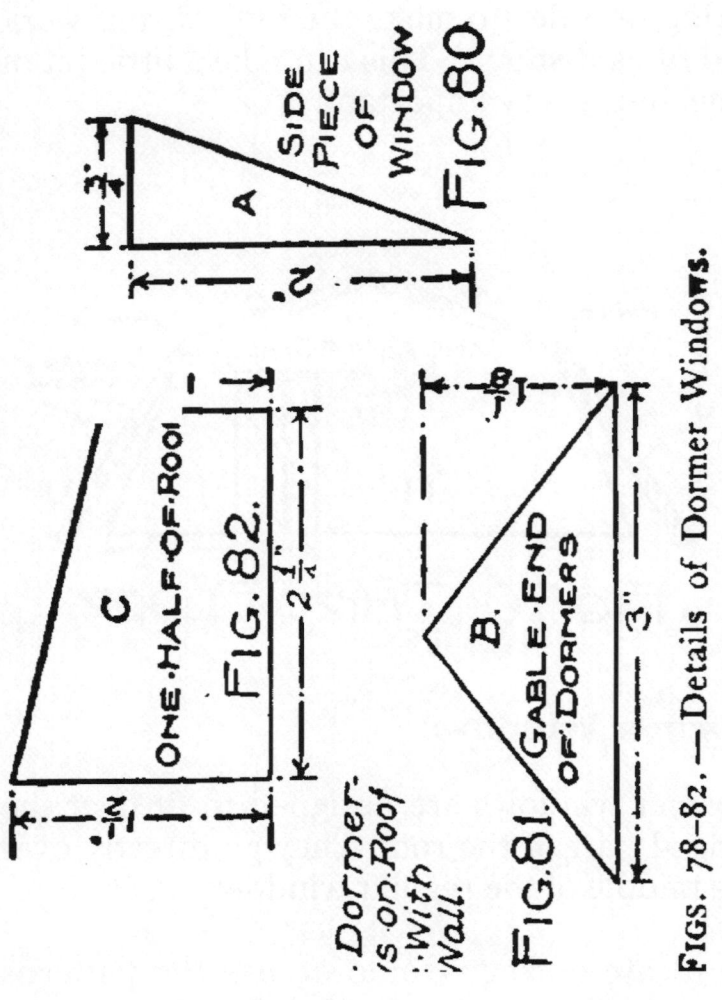

FIGS. 78-82.—Details of Dormer Windows.

48

Once you have all the pieces, you can assemble them in place using small nails or glue. This is shown in Figure 79.

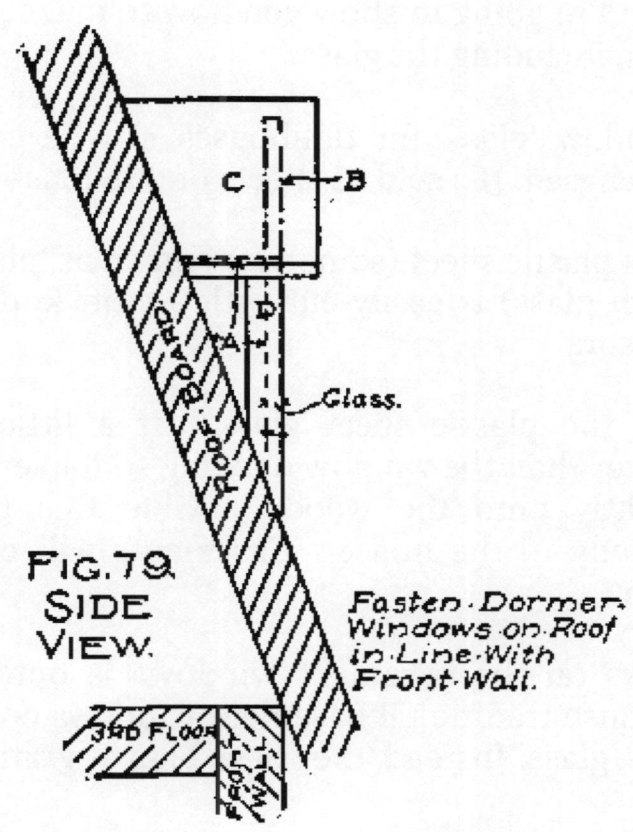

FIG. 79. SIDE VIEW.

Fasten Dormer Windows on Roof in Line With Front Wall.

Windows

Naturally, you can buy pre-made windows but here I'm going to show you how to make your own, including the glass.

Window 'glass' for dollhouses can be easily purchased. It's sold as sheets of thin plastic.

This plastic sheet (sometime known as 'plastic sheet glass) is easily cut with a craft knife or scissors.

Cut the plastic sheet glass just a little bit bigger than the window opening so it overlaps slightly onto the wood. Glue this glass directly to the house. Casements will come later.

Glass on the basement windows is optional because traditional basement windows do not have glass. Instead, they have bars or grating.

Bars or grating can be simulated with toothpicks painted to look like iron. Simply glue them to the house and cover with casements.

Window casements are built directly on the house. These casements go on both the inside and the outside to give the illusion of an entire window. These casements can be built with either thin strip wood, textured lace or card.

Windows are the last thing added to a house because they need to go over the wallpaper, paint or other finishing techniques.

Narrow strips of wood or craft matchsticks placed directly on the plastic sheet glass will give the impression of divided glass.

To give the impression of leaded glass, you can paint these wood strips black to resemble iron.

The included patterns will give you clear measurements you can use to create your window casements.

A simple door can be made with a piece of thin wood or illustration board. A shiny bead works well as a doorknob.

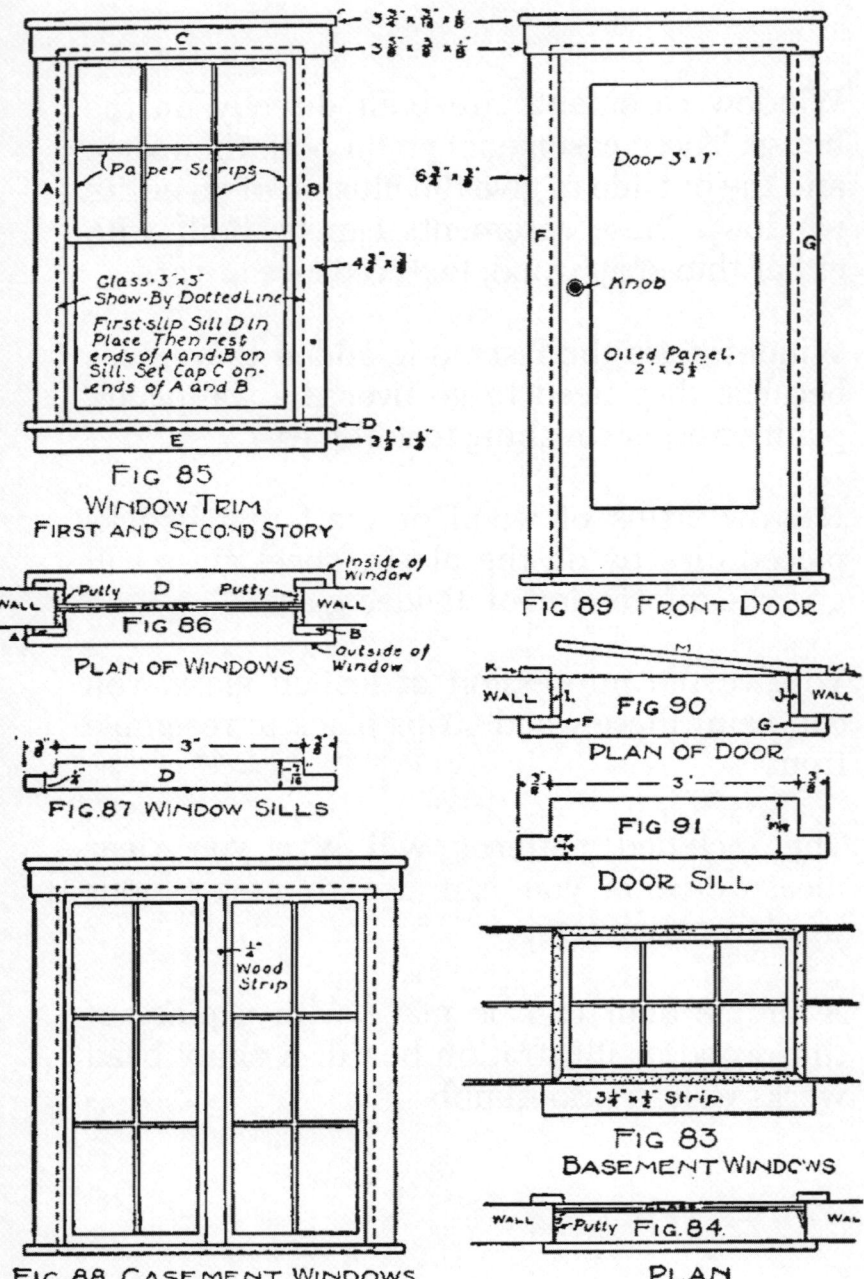

Figs. 83–91. — Details of Windows.

After putting the trim on all of the windows and the doors, cut a number of strips of wood an 1/8 of an inch thick and half an inch wide for outside trimmings, and attach them to each corner of the house.

They should go around the edges of each gable-end, and around the top of the basement.

Buy some narrow molding for the cornice and attach it to the edges of the roof.

Here is where you need to be concerned with making neat miters at the corners. If you don't miter the house at this point, it will not look as neat and finished as it could.

If you don't want to worry about mitering, you can also use strip wood or card. This will give the look of being finished without the advanced woodworking skills.

If you plan on moving the house frequently, consider mounting it on casters or wheels.

Front Steps

The front steps are made the same way you see in figure 76. Stringers, railings and balustrades are made the same as the interior stairs.

These stairs are almost identical to the ones in the interior except for the fact that they are 4" in length.

There will also be a top platform that's about 2 1/2" wide.

Prepare two stringers and 4 balustrades like you did before.

These stringers should only be five steps high. Again, toothpicks can be used for the inner posts while turnings can be used for the balustrades

The back steps are made the same way. They can also be left off entirely.

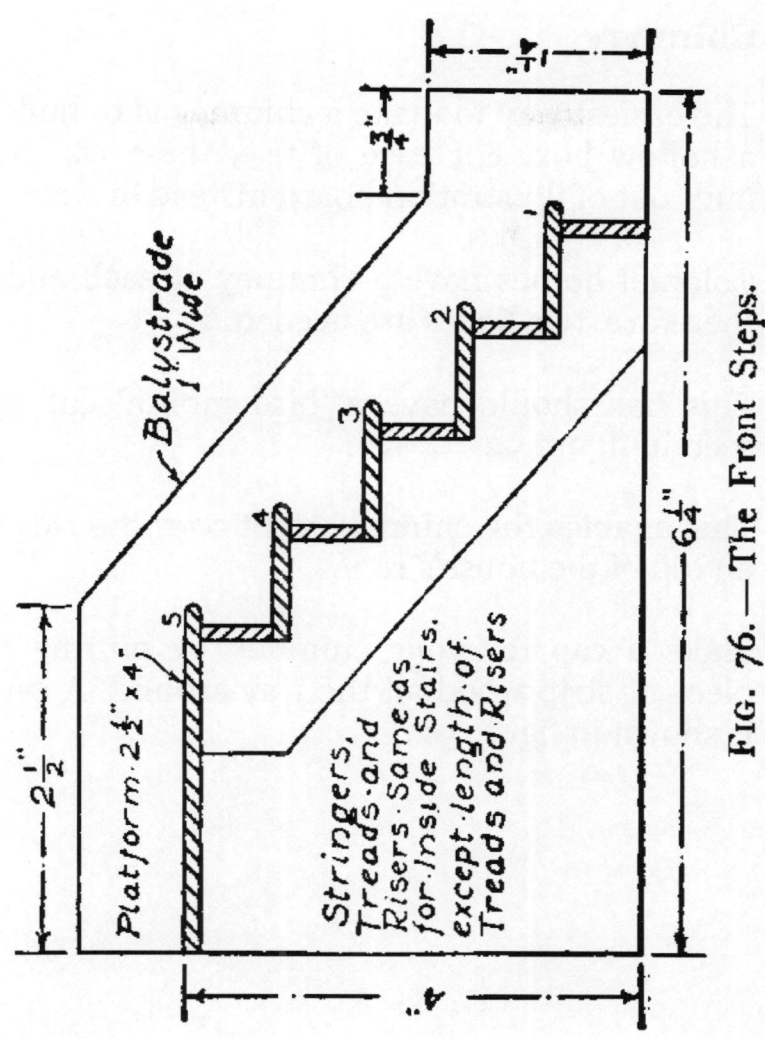

FIG. 76.—The Front Steps.

Chimney

The easiest way to make a chimney is to build a hollow box. For ease of use, these can be built out of illustration board instead of wood.

Colonial homes have a chimney at each end; therefore, two boxes are needed.

This box should have a 'bird mouth' cut as seen in figure 92.

This enables the chimney to fit over the ridge on top of the house's roof.

Make a cap for your chimney by putting a piece of strip wood all the way around. A cap is shown in figure 92.

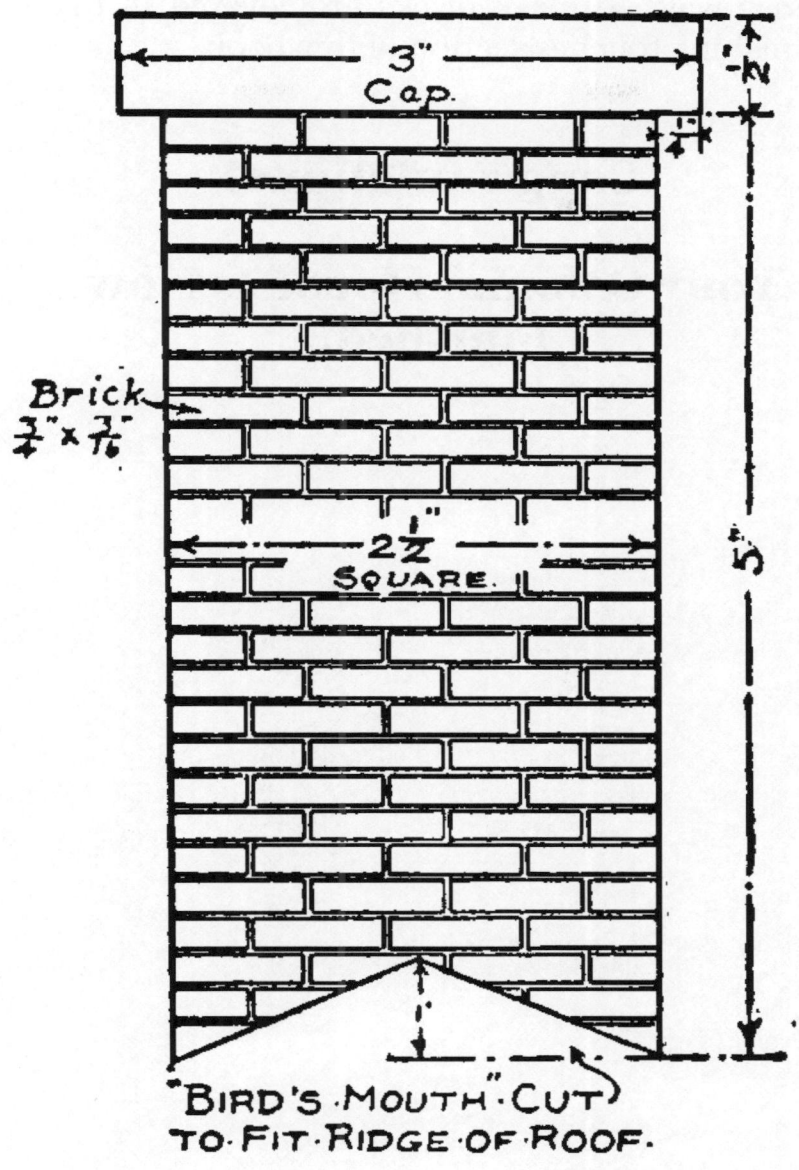

FIG. 92. — Construction of Chimneys.

Easy ways to make bricks are covered in the finishing touches section of this book.

Congratulations!

Your Colonial House Is Now Finished!

Finishing Touches

Now we come to one of the most fun parts about having a dollhouse; the decorating. While this is by no means a comprehensive chapter on decorating, decorating alone could fill a book; this will give you a brief overview on how to finish your dollhouse so you can have one you're proud of.

Floors

There are several options for floors in your dollhouse. Which one you choose will depend on your personal taste.

Using Your Home's Natural Wood

If your dollhouse is made of real wood, then you can you can simply use a craft knife and ruler to score the floor so it looks like planks. When you stain the floor, the stain will naturally collect in these grooves giving the illusion of actual planks.

Popsicle Sticks

To make an inexpensive real wood floor, use popsicle sticks with the round ends cut off. Glue them down, then stain as usual.

Commercial Hardwood Floors

Hardwood floors are available commercially. They are made up thin woods applied to a fabric backing. Since they are genuine, often exotic, woods, they are the most expensive option.

Floor paper
For a more economical alternative to real wood or tile, consider floor paper. Floor paper simulates the look of tile, wood, parquet and more.

Best of all, you can buy whole books of floor paper for the price of the most commercially available hardwood floors.

To see the selection of floor paper available from Dollhouse Devotions, go to:

http://www.thisofferisgreat.com/dd

Carpets and Rugs

Carpets can either be bought commercially or simulated with felt.

Throw rugs can be purchased, created with fancy ribbons, scraps of appropriately textured cloth or old fashioned handkerchiefs.

Tile

Tile has to be small enough in scale both thinness and surface. Polymer clay is an excellent choice for tile because it can be created paper thin.

Plastic dollhouse tile sheets or tiled floor paper are also good options.

Wall Pictures

No home is complete without pictures.

Pictures can be cut out of magazines and then framed with strip wood to give the illusion of a picture in a frame.

These frames can even be embellished with puffy paint or small rhinestones painted a solid color to represent a fancier frame.

You can also use paper frames to show off your mini artwork.

Brick

There are commercial brick kits you can buy to give the illusions of bricks. These kits feature everything from individual clay bricks to stencils and textured paint.

You can also use sand paper cut into brick shapes and painted the appropriate color. These paper bricks have the advantage of being able to turn around corners.

Brick paper can also be used if you want to cover a large area quickly. Like floor paper, brick paper is the most economical alternative. Either you can buy sheets of brick paper or you can purchase a book of floor paper that has the appropriate brick pattern in it.

Shingles

In addition to commercially available shingles, there are many other ways to shingle a house.

Again, sand paper can be used by cutting into the appropriate strips and gluing it into place.

Shingle paper can also be used if you're looking to cover large areas quickly.

Doors

Though doors can be purchased commercially, they can also be made with thin stripwood or board.

These handcrafted doors can be created with pieces of board, strip wood, rhinestones or even puffy paint. Simply apply your embellishments and paint to look like wood or painted wood.

A fabric hinge is easily made by gluing a piece of fabric to both the door and the interior of the door way. This hinge can then be covered with trim, wallpaper or paint.

A shiny bead can serve as doorknob.

Stained Glass

This can easily be replicated by printing out the appropriate patterns on computer transparency paper. When you download the patterns for this dollhouse, you will receive some stained glass patterns in a few days. Size to fit, then print out.

Wallpaper

Wallpaper is one of the most popular ways to finish the inside of a dollhouse. While sheets of wallpaper are available individually, wallpaper books can be purchased at a fraction of the price.

Be sure to check out Dollhouse Devotions' assortment of wallpaper books here:

http://www.thisofferisgreat.com/dd

A Note from Dollhouse Devotions:

If you enjoyed this book, please consider leaving a review.

If you have any suggestions on how to make future books better, you can contact us at:

info@newartspublishing.com

You can also download your free patterns from this book at

http://www.thisofferisgreat.com/dhcolonial

Don't forget to see all our dollhouse books including floor plans and wallpapers.

http://www.thisofferisgreat.com/dd

Printed in Great Britain
by Amazon.co.uk, Ltd.,
Marston Gate.